EASY PIANO ARRANGEMENTS BY
DAN COATES

BROADWAY Today

CONTENTS

Order of cassette

Come To My Garden . . . . . . *The Secret Garden* 4

Favorite Son . . . . *The Will Rogers Follies* . . . 8

What More Can I Say? . . . . . *Falsettos* 13

No More . . . . *The Goodbye Girl* 18

My Unkown Someone . . . . . . *The Will Rogers Follies* . . . 22

With Every Breath I Take . . . . *City Of Angels* 27

You Can Always Count On Me . . *City Of Angels* 31

How Could I Ever Know? . . . . . *The Secret Garden* 36

Cover Photography: Marc Romanelli

DAN COATES

One of today's foremost personalities in the field of printed music, Dan Coates has been providing teachers and professional musicians with quality piano material since 1975. Equally adept in arranging for beginners or accomplished musicians, his Big Note, Easy Piano and Professional Touch arrangements have made a significant contribution to the industry.

Born in Syracuse, New York, Dan began to play piano at age four. By the time he was 15, he'd won a New York State competition for music composers. After high school graduation, he toured the United States, Canada and Europe as an arranger and pianist with the world-famous group "Up With People."

Dan settled in Miami, Florida, where he studied piano with Ivan Davis at the University of Miami while playing professionally throughout southern Florida. To date, his performance credits include appearances on "Murphy Brown," "My Sister Sam" and at the Opening Ceremonies of the 1984 Summer Olympics in Los Angeles. Dan has also accompanied such artists as Dusty Springfield and Charlotte Rae.

In 1982, Dan began his association with Warner Bros. Publications - an association which has produced more than 400 Dan Coates books and sheets. Throughout the year he conducts piano workshops nationwide, during which he demonstrates his popular arrangements.

The LISTEN and PLAY Series features a combination of music book and cassette.

The arrangements have been selected from my Easy Piano Library- and I have performed them exactly as they appear in the book.

These arrangements are intended to bridge the gap between elementary and intermediate levels of performance. You will encounter many of the same challenges you face in early-level classics, sonatinas and contemporary collections.

The tape will help you <u>HEAR</u> the way these pieces were intended to be played. My intention is to provide you with another source to help with any particular problem area you might have...by using your <u>EAR</u>.

Although each of us brings our own individual style and interpretation to a piece of music...I've always found it very helpful to listen to a recording of the piece, and hear how someone else performs the same music.

Have fun with these songs - they represent the talents of some of today's greatest composers.

DAN COATES

COME TO MY GARDEN
From The Broadway Musical "THE SECRET GARDEN"

Lyrics by
MARSHA NORMAN

Music by
LUCY SIMON
Arranged by DAN COATES

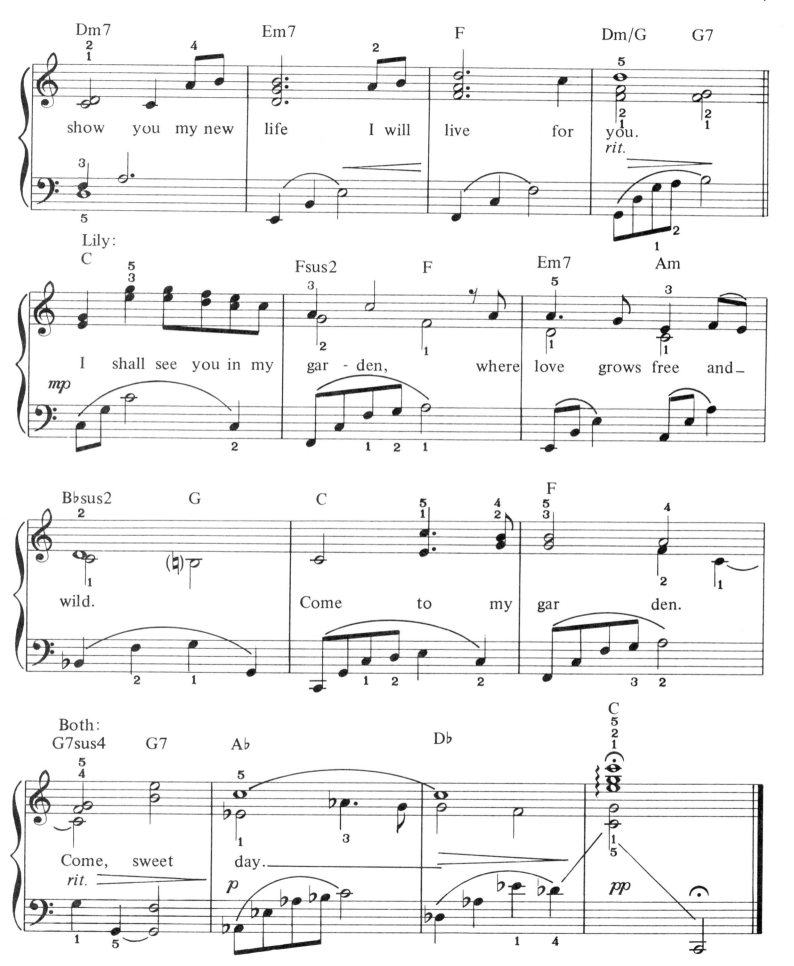

FAVORITE SON
From The Broadway Musical "THE WILL ROGERS FOLLIES"

Music by
CY COLEMAN

Lyrics by
BETTY COMDEN and ADOLPH GREEN
Arranged by DAN COATES

shown. I'll run a clean cam - paign and that will

be my win - ning card. Con - sid - er - ing the kind you've had, well

that won't be too hard.

The el - e - phant

D.S. al Coda

WHAT MORE CAN I SAY?
From The Broadway Musical "FALSETTOS"

Music and Lyrics by
WILLIAM FINN
Arranged by DAN COATES

Moderate Ballad

(Pedal throughout)

It's been hot, al - so ver - y sweet. And I'm not u - su - al - ly in - dis - creet, but when he spar - kles, the earth be - gins to sway. What more can I

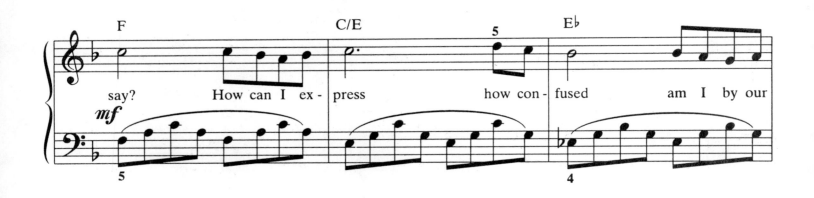

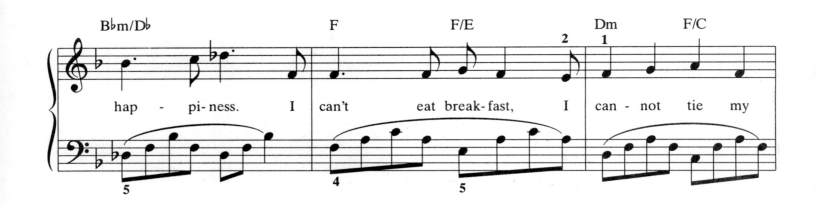

NO MORE
From The Broadway Musical "THE GOODBYE GIRL"

Lyrics by
DAVID ZIPPEL

Music by
MARVIN HAMLISCH
Arranged by DAN COATES

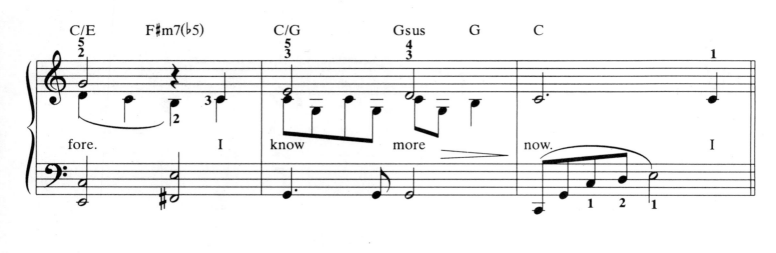

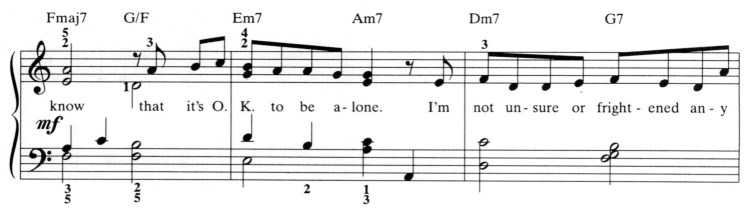

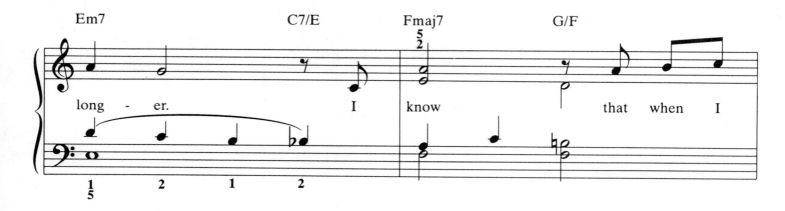

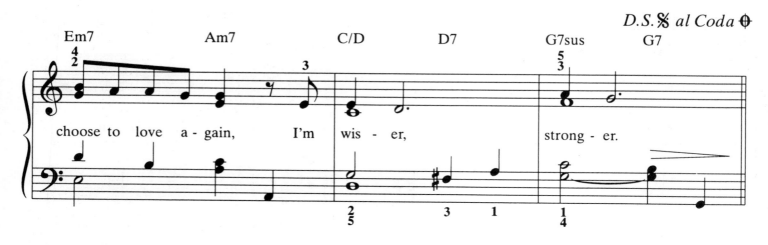

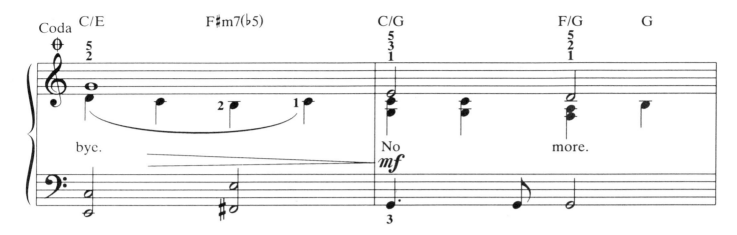

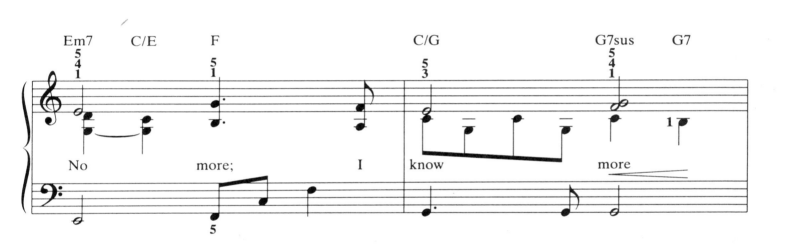

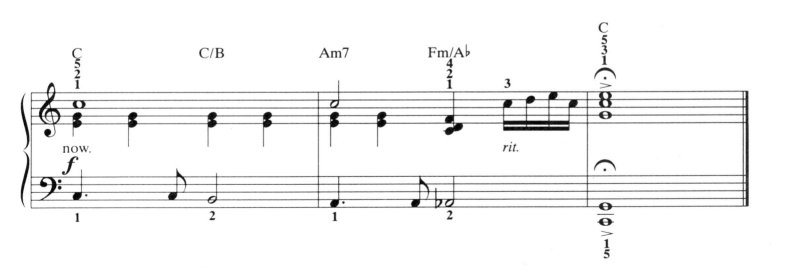

MY UNKNOWN SOMEONE
From The Broadway Musical "THE WILL ROGERS FOLLIES"

Music by
CY COLEMAN

Lyrics by
BETTY COMDEN and ADOLPH GREEN
Arranged by DAN COATES

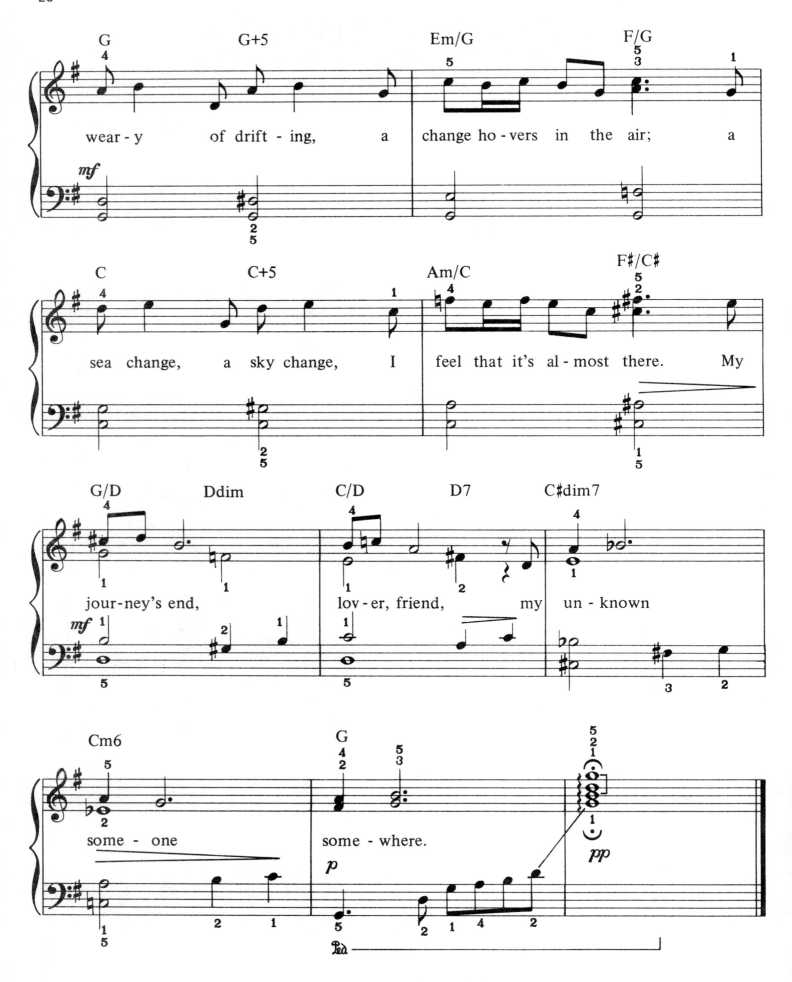

WITH EVERY BREATH I TAKE
From The Broadway Musical "CITY OF ANGELS"

Music by
CY COLEMAN

Lyrics by
DAVID ZIPPEL
Arranged by DAN COATES

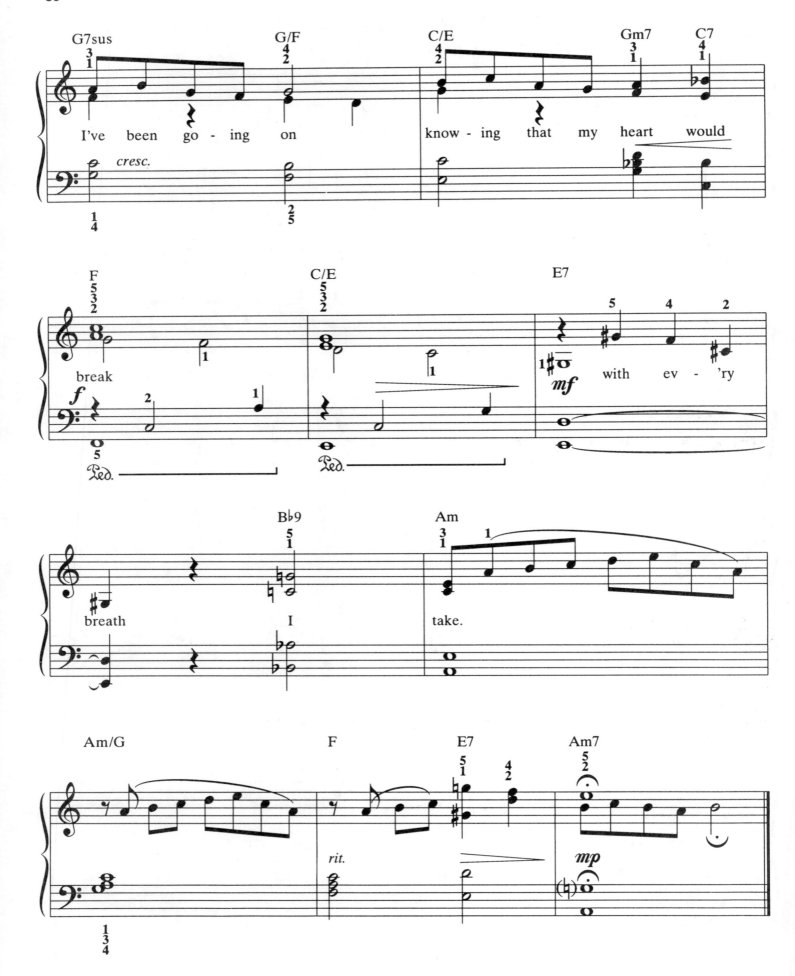

YOU CAN ALWAYS COUNT ON ME
From The Broadway Musical "CITY OF ANGELS"

Music by
CY COLEMAN

Lyrics by
DAVID ZIPPEL
Arranged by DAN COATES

been the "oth - er wo - man" since my pu - ber - ty be - gan, I
Joe who swore he's sin - gle got me sort - a crocked, the beast; I

crashed the jun - ior prom and met the on - ly mar - ried man._____ I'm
woke up on - ly slight - ly shocked that I de - frocked a priest._____ Or

al - ways on top for ro - mance or choc- 'late that's bit - ter - sweet._____⌐
else I at - tract the guys who are long - ing to do my hair._____⌐

To Coda ⊕

1.
You can al - ways count on me._____ A _____

2.
I

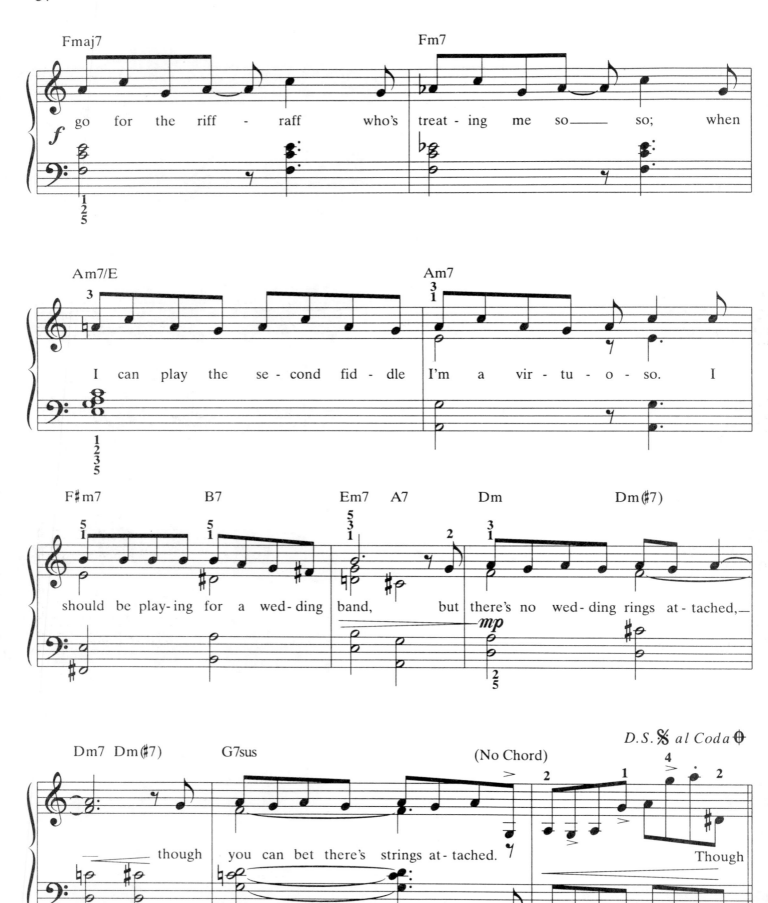

Extra Lyrics:

3. Though my kind of dame no doubt will die out
   Like the dinosaurs,
   You can always count on me.
   I'm solely to blame, my head gives advice
   That my heart ignores.
   I'm my only enemy.
   I choose the kind who cannot introduce
   The girl he's with;
   They're lots of smirking motel clerks
   Who call me Missus Smith.
   But I've made a name with hotel detectives
   Who break down doors.
   Guess who they expect to see? (etc...)

HOW COULD I EVER KNOW?
From The Broadway Musical "THE SECRET GARDEN"

Lyrics by
MARSHA NORMAN

Music by
LUCY SIMON
Arranged by DAN COATES

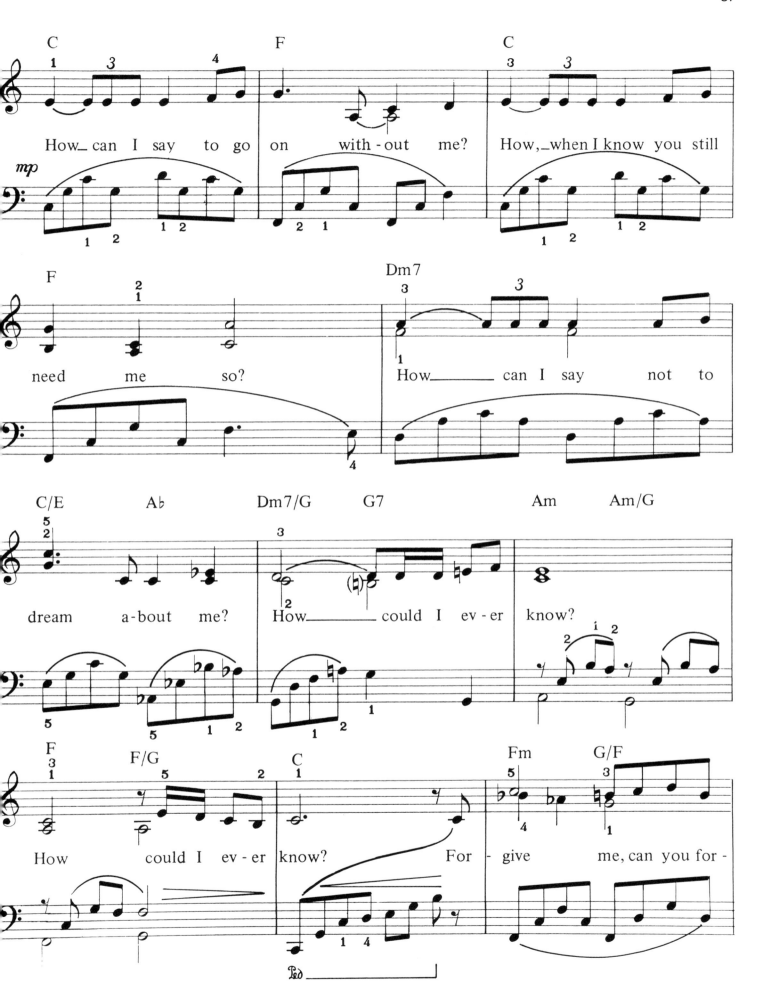